AF317034

PATTERN SEEKERS

The Science Behind Data-Driven Discoveries

Akinfolajimi Bamigbola

TABLE OF CONTENTS

Foreword

We live in a time where data is more abundant than ever. From the moment we wake up to the time we sleep, data is constantly being generated by the technologies we use, the decisions we make, and even the patterns of nature itself. It is no exaggeration to say that we are surrounded by endless streams of information. However, what separates those who simply observe data from those who make revolutionary discoveries is the ability to detect meaningful patterns in the chaos. Data-driven discoveries have shaped industries, redefined entire fields, and solved some of humanity's most complex problems. Whether it's in medicine, where patterns in genetic data have led to breakthrough treatments, or in business, where analyzing customer behavior has given rise to personalized marketing strategies, the science of pattern recognition is at the heart of modern innovation. Yet, the instinct to seek patterns is not something new, it's deeply rooted in our biology and has driven human progress for centuries. The human brain is wired to recognize patterns, and this instinct has been key to our survival. Early humans relied on pattern recognition to identify safe food sources, predict weather changes, and avoid danger. Today, this ancient skill continues to shape how we interact with the world.

In fact, the drive to find patterns has only been amplified in the data-driven age, where sophisticated algorithms and machine learning models can process data on a scale and speed that far surpasses human capability. However, machines alone cannot unlock the full potential of data. It takes a blend of human intuition, creativity, and critical thinking to interpret the patterns revealed by machines and apply them to real-world problems. ***Pattern Seekers: The Science Behind Data-Driven Discoveries*** explores this intricate relationship between humans and data, revealing how we have evolved from relying solely on intuition to using cutting-edge technologies that augment our ability to uncover meaningful patterns. The book is not just about data science as a technical field—it delves into the psychological, cognitive, and ethical dimensions of pattern discovery. It provides insight into how both human and machine-driven pattern recognition has transformed industries, from biology and physics to marketing and urban planning. As you read through the chapters of this book, you'll discover how pattern recognition operates across multiple dimensions.

You'll see how the natural world is filled with mathematical and structural patterns—from fractals in plants to the Fibonacci sequence in seashells— that have inspired some of the most groundbreaking scientific discoveries. You'll also explore how algorithms have become the ultimate pattern seekers in fields like artificial intelligence, where machines now excel in detecting complex, hidden patterns that humans would never notice. Importantly, this book also invites us to consider the ethical implications of pattern recognition in the modern world. The power to detect patterns comes with significant responsibility. Inaccurate or biased patterns can reinforce harmful stereotypes, lead to discrimination in hiring or lending practices, or invade personal privacy. As data science advances, so too must our understanding of how to ethically and responsibly use these discoveries for the betterment of society. Pattern

Seekers is a call to embrace the world of data with curiosity and caution. It encourages us to view pattern recognition as both an ancient human instinct and a modern tool that, when used wisely, can unlock incredible possibilities. Whether you are a data scientist, a curious reader, or someone interested in the future of technology and society, this book will give you the tools to think critically about how patterns shape our world and how we can harness them to create a better future.

Introduction

The Age of Data

We are living in an age where data is the new currency of knowledge. Every click, every purchase, and every movement generates data that can be collected, analyzed, and transformed into insights. From the apps on our smartphones to the massive databases of governments and corporations, the world has become a vast network of information, all waiting to be interpreted and understood. But what gives this mountain of data value? It is the patterns we find within it—the meaningful connections and relationships that turn raw information into actionable intelligence. The ability to detect patterns is not just a modern phenomenon born of big data and machine learning. It is a fundamental part of human nature. For millennia, humans have relied on pattern recognition to survive, evolve, and thrive. Our ancestors used the positions of the stars to navigate the seas, tracked animal behaviors to hunt, and observed the changing seasons to cultivate crops. Even today, we use patterns in language, culture, and behavior to make sense of the world around us. But what has changed is the sheer volume and complexity of the data we now have access to. Thanks to technological advancements, we can process more data than ever before. Machine learning algorithms can scan through massive datasets in seconds, identifying patterns and trends that would be impossible for a human to detect.

Whether it's predicting the spread of a disease, optimizing supply chains, or uncovering fraud, the ability to find patterns in data has become one of the most powerful tools in the modern world. Yet, despite the sophistication of our algorithms, the human instinct to seek patterns remains at the core of every discovery. What makes this process so fascinating is not just the data itself, but the interaction between human curiosity and machine-driven analysis. Data scientists, researchers, and professionals across every industry are working in tandem with these tools, using a blend of intuition, experience, and technology to turn data into meaningful insights. This book, ***Pattern Seekers: The Science Behind Data-Driven Discoveries***, takes you on a journey through the science and pattern recognition. It explores the history of how humans have been identifying patterns for centuries and how modern technologies have amplified this ability beyond what we once thought possible. Along the way, we'll examine how patterns shape our understanding of everything from natural phenomena like weather patterns and biological systems to social trends, business insights, and artificial intelligence.

In the chapters ahead, we'll dive into topics like how the brain is wired for pattern recognition, how algorithms mimic human intuition to detect patterns, and the ethical considerations that arise when we use data to make critical decisions. You'll see how pattern recognition in data is being applied across industries, from healthcare and finance to marketing and urban planning. Each chapter reveals the intricate process of transforming raw data into valuable insights, showing how both humans and machines work together to seek order from chaos. But this isn't just a book for data scientists or tech enthusiasts. It's for anyone curious about how the world around them operates at its most fundamental level. Patterns are everywhere—in nature, in business, and in the way we interact with one another. Understanding these patterns allows us to predict outcomes, make smarter decisions, and ultimately shape the future. As you read through this book, you'll come to see that pattern-seeking is not just a technical skill; it's a mindset. It's about being open to the unknown, asking the right questions, and seeing beyond the surface to uncover hidden connections. Whether you are a professional working with data every day or someone just beginning to explore the possibilities, this book will provide you with the tools and insights to become a more effective pattern seeker in the age of data.

"The world is full of obvious things which nobody by any chance ever observes."
– Arthur Conan Doyle, The Hound of the Baskervilles

"Patterns are not things we see, but things we use."

– Peter Senge

"The universe is full of magical things, patiently waiting for our wits to grow sharper."

– Eden Phillpotts

"Without data, you're just another person with an opinion."

– W. Edwards Deming

"In the data, as in life, patterns emerge only if we look for them."

– Anonymous

Chapter 1

The Nature of Patterns

The world is full of patterns, both natural and artificial. From the arrangement of leaves on a tree to the rise and fall of stock prices, patterns shape much of what we see, feel, and experience. But what exactly are patterns, and why are they so critical to data science? At its core, a pattern is a regular, repeating sequence or structure that emerges from data or observations. In nature, patterns manifest in phenomena like the spirals of seashells or the branching of rivers. In the realm of human-made systems, patterns exist in the flow of traffic, the rise and fall of economic markets, and even in the rhythm of our daily routines. Identifying these patterns allows us to make sense of complex environments, predict future outcomes, and respond in meaningful ways. Patterns are essential to data science because they reveal insights that raw data alone cannot.

Without pattern recognition, data would remain a chaotic mix of information with little meaning. In data science, the goal is to uncover these hidden structures and regularities that can lead to actionable insights. By recognizing patterns, we can predict future trends, understand customer behaviors, detect anomalies in network security, and much more. However, identifying patterns is not always simple. Data is often noisy, incomplete, or overwhelming in volume. In many cases, what appears to be a pattern may be random noise, while real, meaningful patterns might be hidden deep within layers of data. One of the great challenges in modern data science is learning how to distinguish between randomness and significant patterns. As data continues to grow in complexity and size, our ability to detect patterns becomes even more important. Through algorithms and advanced computing, we can now recognize patterns that were once invisible, helping to solve problems across fields like healthcare, finance, and environmental science.

Defining Patterns: Order in Chaos

At the simplest level, a pattern is a regular, repeating sequence or structure. It's a recognizable form or order that emerges from data or observations. In nature, patterns might manifest as the spiral shells of a nautilus, the veins in a leaf, or the rhythmic cycles of the seasons. In the world of mathematics, patterns can be found in sequences of numbers, geometric shapes, or algebraic formulas. And in the digital age, patterns exist in the vast seas of data we collect every second—from social media interactions to financial transactions to biometric data. Patterns are valuable because they help us make sense of complexity. In a world full of noise and chaos, patterns give us structure. They allow us to predict future behavior based on past occurrences. This predictive power is at the heart of data science, enabling everything from weather forecasts to personalized product recommendations. However, identifying patterns is not always straightforward. Data is often messy, incomplete, and complex. What appears to be a pattern may be a coincidence, while true patterns can be buried deep within layers of noise. The challenge of data science is to distinguish between random fluctuations and meaningful signals—a task that becomes more difficult as the volume and complexity of data continue to grow.

Historical Perspectives on Pattern Recognition

Pattern recognition is not a new phenomenon. Long before the advent of modern technology, humans were identifying patterns in the world around them. Our ancestors relied on pattern recognition to survive. They learned to recognize the changing patterns of the seasons, the migration habits of animals, and the phases of the moon. These patterns were essential for predicting weather, finding food, and navigating the natural world. In ancient Egypt, farmers observed that the annual flooding of the Nile followed a predictable pattern. This observation allowed them to plan their agricultural activities, ensuring a steady supply of food. Similarly, in ancient Greece, philosophers like Pythagoras and Euclid explored patterns in mathematics, laying the groundwork for geometry and number theory. The famous Fibonacci sequence—where each number is the sum of the two preceding numbers—is a mathematical pattern that appears in nature, from the arrangement of sunflower seeds to the spirals of a seashell. In astronomy, the discovery of regular patterns in the movements of celestial bodies led to the development of calendars, navigation techniques, and eventually, the scientific revolution. By observing the stars, early astronomers identified patterns that allowed them to predict eclipses, chart the seasons, and even navigate across oceans. These early examples illustrate the power of pattern recognition. By understanding the underlying structure of natural and mathematical systems, humans have been able to make predictions, solve problems, and innovate. But as data has become more abundant and complex, the tools we use to detect patterns have evolved as well.

Patterns in the Age of Data Science

In today's data-driven world, pattern recognition is more important than ever. We now have access to massive amounts of data, far more than any human could process manually. As a result, we rely on computers and algorithms to help us detect patterns in this sea of information. Data science is the field that combines mathematics, statistics, and computer science to make sense of large datasets. One of the core tasks of data science is identifying patterns that can be used to make predictions or draw insights. For example, businesses use data science to analyze customer behavior and forecast sales trends. Healthcare professionals use it to identify risk factors for diseases and develop personalized treatment plans. In the financial sector, data scientists detect fraudulent transactions by identifying patterns in spending behavior. The process of pattern recognition in data science often begins with data preprocessing. Raw data is rarely in a form that can be easily analyzed. It is often incomplete, inconsistent, or noisy. Data scientists spend a significant amount of time cleaning and transforming data, ensuring that it is accurate and suitable for analysis. This might involve removing outliers, filling in missing values, or normalizing data to ensure that it is comparable across different sources. Once the data is preprocessed, data scientists use statistical and machine learning techniques to identify patterns. Supervised learning algorithms can detect patterns by learning from labeled datasets, where the outcome is already known. For example, a supervised learning algorithm might be trained on a dataset of customer purchases to predict which products a customer is likely to buy next. Unsupervised learning algorithms, on the other hand, identify patterns without prior knowledge of the outcome. These algorithms can detect hidden patterns or groupings in data, such as clusters of customers with similar buying habits.

The Role of Patterns in Machine Learning

In the context of machine learning, pattern recognition is fundamental. Machine learning algorithms are designed to detect patterns in data and use these patterns to make decisions or predictions. The better an algorithm is at recognizing patterns, the more accurate its predictions will be. One of the most common forms of pattern recognition in machine learning is classification. Classification algorithms are trained to recognize patterns in labelled data and assign new data points to predefined categories. For example, a classification algorithm might be trained on a dataset of images to recognize whether an image contains a cat or a dog. The algorithm learns the distinguishing features of each category—such as the shape of the ears or the texture of the fur—and uses these patterns to classify new images. Another important task in machine learning is clustering, which involves identifying groups or clusters within a dataset. Clustering algorithms are often used in marketing to segment customers based on their behavior or preferences. By detecting patterns in purchasing behavior, businesses can create targeted marketing campaigns for different customer segments, improving engagement and sales. Pattern recognition also plays a key role in anomaly detection. In many industries, identifying outliers or unusual patterns is critical for detecting problems before they escalate. For example, in cybersecurity, anomaly detection algorithms can identify patterns of network traffic that deviate from the norm, signaling a potential security breach. Similarly, in finance, detecting anomalous spending patterns can help identify fraudulent transactions.

Order vs. Chaos: The Fine Line Between Patterns and Noise

One of the biggest challenges in pattern recognition is distinguishing between genuine patterns and random noise. Not every correlation is meaningful, and not every trend is a sign of something significant. In some cases, what appears to be a pattern may simply be the result of chance or coincidence. This phenomenon, known as overfitting, occurs when a model detects patterns in the training data that do not generalize to new, unseen data. Overfitting can lead to highly accurate predictions on historical data, but poor performance when applied to real-world situations. To avoid overfitting, data scientists use techniques such as cross-validation, which involves testing a model on different subsets of data to ensure that it performs well across a variety of scenarios. On the other hand, some patterns are hidden so deeply within complex datasets that they may initially appear as noise. One famous example of this is the discovery of the cosmic microwave background radiation, which was initially dismissed as interference. However, upon closer analysis, scientists realized that this radiation was a remnant from the Big Bang, providing crucial evidence for the origins of the universe. This highlights the importance of not dismissing data too quickly—sometimes what appears to be random may hold the key to groundbreaking discoveries.

The Future of Pattern Recognition: Beyond Human Capabilities

As the volume of data continues to grow, the future of pattern recognition will increasingly rely on artificial intelligence and machine learning. These technologies have already revolutionized industries such as healthcare, finance, and logistics, and their potential is only beginning to be realized. In healthcare, for instance, AI algorithms can detect patterns in genetic data that may indicate a predisposition to certain diseases. In finance, machine learning models are used to analyze market data in real time, identifying patterns that human traders might miss. In climate science, AI is helping researchers detect patterns in vast datasets to predict changes in weather patterns and understand the impacts of climate change. The ability to recognize patterns on a large scale is also driving advances in autonomous systems. Self-driving cars, for example, rely on pattern recognition to navigate roads, avoid obstacles, and make decisions in real time. By analyzing data from sensors, cameras, and GPS, these systems detect patterns in traffic, road conditions, and pedestrian behavior, allowing them to operate safely in complex environments. However, as AI becomes more powerful, it also raises ethical concerns. The ability to detect patterns in personal data—such as shopping habits, social interactions, or online behavior—can be used for targeted advertising, surveillance, or even manipulation. It is important that as we continue to develop these technologies, we do so with a focus on transparency, fairness, and ethical responsibility. Patterns are the foundation of our understanding of the world. From the natural rhythms of the universe to the digital footprints we leave behind, patterns help us navigate complexity, make predictions, and solve problems. In the age of data science, the ability to recognize patterns is more important than ever, driving innovation in fields as diverse as healthcare, finance, and artificial intelligence. As we move into the next chapter, we will explore how the human brain has evolved to recognize patterns, and how this innate ability has shaped our understanding of the world and continues to influence modern data science.

Chapter 2

The Human Brain: A Natural Pattern Seeker

The human brain is an extraordinary organ, processing immense amounts of information every second. One of its most fundamental functions is pattern recognition, the ability to detect regularities, structures, and sequences in our environment. From recognizing familiar faces and identifying speech to predicting movements or outcomes, our brains are naturally wired to seek patterns. This skill has been crucial for human survival, helping our ancestors navigate a complex world by recognizing and predicting changes in their environment.

Pattern recognition is not just about survival, though. It shapes much of our everyday lives, from how we learn new languages to how we solve problems or understand visual stimuli. The brain does this by processing sensory inputs—sights, sounds, smells, and more—and comparing them to stored information to detect familiar patterns. This process often occurs without conscious thought, allowing us to react quickly to familiar situations. However, the brain's reliance on patterns also leads to cognitive shortcuts or biases, which can sometimes cause us to see patterns that don't exist.

In this chapter, we will explore the intricate ways the brain recognizes patterns and how it has evolved to do so efficiently. We'll also delve into how cognitive biases, like confirmation bias or the clustering illusion, can distort our pattern recognition abilities, causing us to draw incorrect conclusions from data. Understanding these tendencies is crucial, especially as we rely more heavily on data-driven decisions.

Additionally, the chapter examines how our natural pattern-seeking abilities have influenced the development of artificial intelligence (AI) and machine learning. These technologies are designed to mimic the brain's capacity for detecting patterns, but on a much larger scale. From image recognition to natural language processing, machines are increasingly taking on the role of pattern seekers in the modern world.

The Evolutionary Roots of Pattern Recognition

Pattern recognition is not just a learned skill; it's deeply embedded in our biology. From an evolutionary standpoint, the ability to detect patterns was essential for early humans to survive. Our ancestors relied on this skill to find food, avoid predators, and navigate complex environments. Recognizing the changing patterns of the seasons allowed early humans to track animal migrations, plan agricultural activities, and prepare for harsh weather conditions.

In essence, the brain's ability to detect patterns helped humans predict what would happen next—an invaluable survival tool. This predictive power meant the difference between life and death. Early humans who could recognize a pattern in the way animals moved were better hunters. Those who could detect the subtle cues in nature that signaled an approaching storm were better equipped to seek shelter in time.

This pattern-seeking behavior has not only ensured our survival but also paved the way for human progress. The ability to observe and understand patterns in the stars, tides, and seasons allowed ancient civilizations to develop sophisticated calendars, navigation systems, and agricultural techniques. Today, these same skills are applied in modern contexts like scientific discovery, technological innovation, and business strategy.

How the Brain Recognizes Patterns

The brain is an incredibly efficient pattern recognition machine. It operates by constantly analyzing sensory input—whether it's visual, auditory, or tactile—and comparing it to stored information to identify familiar patterns. This process happens in the background, often without conscious thought. For example, when you look at a friend's face, your brain instantly recognizes them based on the patterns of their facial features. You don't have to actively think about their eye shape or smile; your brain does the work automatically.

Neuroscientists have identified several regions in the brain that are responsible for pattern recognition. The visual cortex, located at the back of the brain, processes visual information and helps us recognize objects, faces, and environments. The auditory cortex, located in the temporal lobes, processes sound and allows us to recognize voices, music, and language patterns. Other areas, like the prefrontal cortex, are involved in higher-order thinking and help us detect more abstract patterns, such as those found in math or logic.

One of the key features of the brain's pattern recognition ability is its efficiency. The brain doesn't process every piece of information it encounters in detail. Instead, it uses heuristics—mental shortcuts based on prior experience—to quickly identify familiar patterns. These shortcuts allow us to respond rapidly to our environment, but they also come with trade-offs. While heuristics help us navigate the world more efficiently, they can sometimes lead to errors or cognitive biases.

Cognitive Biases and Pattern Recognition

Although the brain's ability to detect patterns is one of its greatest strengths, it is not without its limitations. In some cases, the brain's pattern recognition machinery can go awry, leading us to see patterns where none exist. This phenomenon is known as apophenia, the tendency to perceive meaningful connections between unrelated things. A common example of apophenia is seeing shapes in clouds or faces in inanimate objects, like the famous "face on Mars" image captured by NASA.

Cognitive biases also play a significant role in how we recognize patterns. One of the most well-known biases is confirmation bias, where individuals favor information that confirms their pre-existing beliefs while ignoring evidence that contradicts them. In the context of pattern recognition, confirmation bias can lead us to selectively interpret data in a way that reinforces our expectations, even if the pattern we think we've identified isn't real. This is particularly problematic in fields like science and business, where decisions based on faulty pattern recognition can have serious consequences.

Another bias closely related to pattern recognition is the clustering illusion—the tendency to see clusters in random data. This bias is often seen in gambling, where people perceive patterns in the outcomes of random events, like the roll of a die or the spin of a roulette wheel. Despite knowing that each event is independent and that no pattern exists, the brain seeks order in the chaos, leading to erroneous conclusions about future outcomes.

Understanding these cognitive biases is crucial for anyone working with data or engaging in problem-solving. By being aware of how our brains can misinterpret information, we can take steps to minimize bias and make more accurate decisions.

Intuition: The Subconscious Pattern Seeker

Another remarkable aspect of the brain's pattern recognition ability is its connection to intuition. Intuition can be thought of as the brain's subconscious ability to recognize patterns based on past experiences and apply them to new situations. When you have a "gut feeling" about something, your brain is drawing on stored patterns from previous encounters and using them to make a quick decision, often without you being consciously aware of it.

In fields like medicine, seasoned doctors rely on intuition to diagnose conditions based on patterns they've encountered in previous patients. Similarly, experienced investors may develop an intuitive sense of market trends after years of observing financial patterns. This type of pattern recognition operates beneath the surface of conscious thought, but it can be a powerful tool for decision-making.

However, just like with cognitive biases, intuition isn't foolproof. It's based on the brain's pattern recognition systems, which can be influenced by incomplete or misleading information. While intuition can be valuable in many situations, it's essential to validate gut feelings with data, especially in fields like science, finance, and healthcare.

The Brain and Artificial Intelligence: Mimicking Human Pattern Recognition

The study of how the brain recognizes patterns has significantly influenced the development of artificial intelligence (AI) and machine learning. In fact, many AI algorithms are designed to mimic the brain's ability to detect patterns, albeit on a much larger scale. Neural networks, a key component of modern machine learning systems, are inspired by the structure of the human brain, with layers of interconnected nodes functioning similarly to neurons.

These neural networks excel at tasks that require pattern recognition, such as image classification, speech recognition, and language translation. For example, AI systems trained on vast datasets of images can recognize faces, objects, and even emotions by identifying the subtle patterns in pixel arrangements. Similarly, natural language processing (NLP) systems can detect patterns in text, allowing them to understand context, translate languages, or even generate human-like conversation.

While AI systems can process data far more quickly and accurately than the human brain, they still rely on the same fundamental principles of pattern recognition. However, unlike humans, AI doesn't possess intuition or the ability to draw on past experiences in the same way. AI's pattern recognition abilities are purely data-driven, which can lead to challenges when working with ambiguous or incomplete data.

Conclusion: A Natural Born Pattern Seeker

The human brain's ability to detect patterns is one of the most fundamental aspects of our cognition. From the earliest days of human evolution to modern technological advancements, pattern recognition has shaped the way we understand and interact with the world. Our brain's natural ability to seek out order in chaos has allowed us to make sense of complex environments, predict future events, and innovate in ways that have driven human progress.

However, this pattern-seeking ability is not without its pitfalls. Cognitive biases and the limitations of our intuition can lead us to see patterns that aren't there or misinterpret the data before us. As we continue to advance in fields like AI and machine learning, understanding how our brains recognize patterns—and how we can improve upon this skill—will be crucial to unlocking the full potential of data-driven discovery.

In the next chapter, we will explore how raw data is transformed into valuable insights, delving into the processes that enable us to identify and extract meaningful patterns from the vast amounts of information we collect.

Chapter 3

From Data to Insight: The Pattern Discovery Process

In the digital age, data has become the new oil—an immensely valuable resource that, when processed correctly, can drive innovation and improve decision-making across industries. However, like crude oil, raw data in its unprocessed form is of limited value. It is only through systematic refining, cleaning, and analyzing that data becomes useful and transforms into actionable insights. The journey from raw data to meaningful insights begins with data collection. In today's interconnected world, data can come from countless sources: customer transactions, social media activity, sensors, and much more. Once collected, this raw data often contains errors, inconsistencies, and missing values, which need to be addressed through data cleaning and preparation. Cleaning ensures that the data is accurate and reliable, while preparation standardizes formats and structures, making it suitable for analysis. The next step is data transformation and integration, which involves converting data into a format that can be effectively analyzed and integrating it from multiple sources to provide a more comprehensive dataset. By transforming data, analysts can create new features that highlight hidden patterns, and integrating data from various sources enhances the richness of the dataset. Once the data is ready, it undergoes exploration and visualization. Analysts use statistical techniques and visual tools like charts, graphs, and plots to reveal initial patterns and trends in the data. This stage allows for the discovery of correlations, outliers, and emerging relationships that might guide deeper analysis. The core of the process is pattern detection, where algorithms and models are applied to uncover significant patterns in the data. Techniques like clustering, classification, and anomaly detection allow analysts to segment data, predict outcomes, and identify unusual behaviors. Finally, insights are generated through interpretation and communication. The patterns discovered must be translated into actionable recommendations, simplifying complex data into insights that drive decision-making. This final stage bridges the gap between data analysis and strategic action.

The Data Deluge: Challenges and Opportunities

The rise of digital technology has ushered in an era of unprecedented data production. We live in a world where every online transaction, social media interaction, sensor reading, and smartphone activity generates data. This phenomenon, known as big data, comes with three major characteristics: volume, velocity, and variety. The sheer quantity of data produced globally each day can be overwhelming, and the speed at which it is generated requires real-time processing capabilities. Moreover, the variety of data, ranging from structured databases to unstructured text and multimedia, presents challenges for analysis.

Although the data deluge can be intimidating, it also offers enormous potential. When properly harnessed, this data provides insights that were once inaccessible. Businesses can gain an intimate understanding of consumer behavior, governments can optimize public services, and scientists can accelerate research by tapping into large datasets. The key to unlocking this potential lies in navigating the pattern discovery process—a systematic approach that transforms raw data into actionable intelligence.

The Pattern Discovery Process: An Overview

The transformation of raw data into insights involves several critical stages. First, data collection is essential, where relevant data is gathered from a variety of sources, such as databases, web analytics, sensors, and public datasets. Once collected, the data typically contains errors, inconsistencies, and redundancies, which must be addressed through data cleaning and preparation. This step ensures that the data is of high quality and suitable for analysis.

Following data cleaning, the data is transformed and integrated, meaning it is standardized and converted into a format appropriate for further analysis. Data from multiple sources may be combined to provide a more comprehensive dataset. After these initial steps, the process moves into data exploration and visualization, where analysts use statistical tools and graphical representations to uncover initial patterns, trends, and correlations. At this stage, analysts form hypotheses and determine which aspects of the data deserve deeper investigation.

The core of the pattern discovery process is pattern detection and analysis, where algorithms and models are applied to extract insights. These patterns are then interpreted and translated into actionable insights that can inform decision-making, shape strategies, and spark innovation. Each of these stages requires a mix of technical skills, domain knowledge, and analytical thinking to uncover hidden relationships within the data.

Data Collection: Laying the Foundation

The first step in transforming data into insight is collecting the right information. Data collection involves identifying relevant sources that can contribute to solving the problem or answering the question at hand. Depending on the domain, data can come from internal company databases, customer transaction records, online interactions, or external sources like social media feeds, sensors, and publicly available datasets.

For example, consider a retail company that collects data from its in-store transactions, online purchases, loyalty programs, and customer service interactions. In scientific research, data might come from controlled laboratory experiments, satellite images, or genomic sequencing. Collecting data from diverse sources allows analysts to build a complete picture of the situation they are investigating.

However, not all data is equally useful. It is critical to ensure that the collected data is relevant to the analysis, reliable, and accurate. The timeliness of the data is also crucial, particularly in fields were information changes rapidly, such as financial markets. Moreover, the process of data collection must adhere to legal and ethical standards, especially when it involves personal data. Issues of privacy, consent, and compliance with regulations like GDPR must be carefully considered to ensure the responsible use of data.

Data Cleaning and Preparation: Ensuring Quality

After data collection, the next step is to clean and prepare the data. Raw data often contains errors, missing values, and inconsistencies that can compromise the validity of the analysis. Data cleaning addresses these issues to ensure that the dataset is accurate, complete, and ready for analysis. Incomplete records may need to be removed, or missing values may need to be imputed using statistical techniques.

Errors in the dataset, such as typos, incorrect values, or inconsistent formatting, are also corrected during this stage. For example, different datasets might represent dates in various formats, which can cause problems during analysis. By standardizing the format, data scientists ensure consistency across the dataset. Similarly, duplicate entries are identified and removed to prevent skewed results.

Outliers—data points that deviate significantly from the rest—also require attention. Sometimes outliers are errors that need to be corrected or excluded, but in other cases, they represent important insights that warrant further investigation. The goal of data cleaning is to ensure that the data is both reliable and ready for analysis, as the quality of the data directly impacts the validity of the conclusions drawn.

Data Transformation and Integration: Creating a Unified Dataset

Data transformation involves converting data into a format that can be effectively analyzed. This may involve normalizing data to ensure that variables are on a common scale, encoding categorical variables as numerical values, or creating new features that capture additional dimensions of the data. Feature engineering, for example, allows data scientists to derive new variables from existing data, which can reveal hidden patterns or relationships. For instance, converting timestamps into time-based features, like day of the week or hour of the day, can help identify time-based patterns in sales or customer activity.

In many cases, data must be integrated from multiple sources to create a unified dataset. For example, a company might combine data from its website, sales system, and customer support interactions to gain a holistic view of customer behavior. Data integration presents several challenges, including resolving schema differences between datasets, matching records across sources, and ensuring consistency between integrated datasets.

This step of transforming and integrating data ensures that it is ready for deeper analysis, enabling data scientists to uncover patterns that span multiple variables and sources.

Data Exploration and Visualization: Unveiling Hidden Structures

Once the data has been cleaned, transformed, and integrated, the next step is to explore it. Data exploration involves using summary statistics and visualization techniques to gain a better understanding of the dataset. Descriptive statistics, such as averages, medians, and standard deviations, can reveal the overall distribution of the data and help analysts identify patterns and relationships. Correlation analysis, for instance, can indicate how two variables are related, which is crucial for understanding the structure of the dataset.

Data visualization plays a key role in this stage, as it allows analysts to see patterns that might not be immediately obvious from numerical data alone. Scatter plots, histograms, heat maps, and line charts are common visualization tools used to explore data. Visual representations make it easier to detect outliers, clusters, trends, and correlations that would otherwise be difficult to identify.

Data exploration helps form initial hypotheses about the data, guiding analysts toward the most promising areas for further investigation.

Pattern Detection and Analysis: Extracting Insights

After data exploration, the pattern detection phase begins. This is where advanced analytical techniques and algorithms are applied to extract meaningful patterns from the data. The methods used vary depending on the type of data and the goals of the analysis. For instance, clustering algorithms can group similar data points together, revealing segments or clusters within the data. This is particularly useful in market segmentation, were businesses group customers with similar preferences.

Classification algorithms, on the other hand, assign data points to predefined categories. In healthcare, for example, classification models can be used to predict whether a patient is likely to develop a certain condition based on their medical history. Other techniques, such as time series analysis, examine data points collected over time to identify trends or cycles, making them valuable for forecasting.

Anomaly detection algorithms are used to identify outliers or data points that deviate from the norm, which can be critical for detecting fraud or identifying errors in systems. The key to successful pattern detection lies in selecting the right algorithm or model for the specific problem being addressed.

Machine learning plays a pivotal role in this phase. By training algorithms on historical data, machine learning models can make predictions or uncover previously hidden patterns. For example, predictive models might forecast future sales based on past trends, while deep learning algorithms excel at recognizing patterns in complex data, such as images or natural language.

Interpretation and Insight Generation: From Patterns to Action

Once patterns are detected, the final step is interpreting the findings and translating them into actionable insights. This involves validating the results to ensure that the patterns are not due to random chance and are statistically significant. Contextualizing the results is also critical; analysts must consider the broader business or scientific context to draw meaningful conclusions.

Effective communication of insights is equally important. Data scientists often present their findings to stakeholders, who may not have the technical expertise to understand the intricacies of the analysis. Therefore, simplifying complex data through data storytelling, clear visuals, and straightforward recommendations is essential. This ensures that the insights derived from the analysis can be understood and acted upon.

In healthcare, for instance, insights from data might lead to personalized treatment plans for patients, while in business, they could inform marketing strategies or operational improvements. The goal of the entire pattern discovery process is not just to identify patterns but to use them to make informed, strategic decisions.

Conclusion: Unlocking the Power of Data

The journey from data to insight is a complex yet rewarding process. By collecting, cleaning, transforming, and analyzing data, we can unlock the hidden patterns that provide a deeper understanding of the world around us. The pattern discovery process empowers businesses, researchers, and decision-makers to make data-driven decisions, turning raw information into knowledge and, ultimately, action.

In the next chapter, we will explore how algorithms, particularly machine learning, have revolutionized pattern recognition, enabling us to uncover patterns that were previously invisible and transforming how we interact with data in the modern world.

Chapter 4

Algorithms: The Ultimate Pattern Seekers

As the digital world expands, the data we generate grows exponentially. This vast sea of information contains hidden patterns, but the sheer volume and complexity make it impossible for humans to process alone. Algorithms, however, are designed to efficiently detect patterns within large datasets. These mathematical tools are the backbone of modern data science, capable of uncovering relationships, trends, and anomalies that would otherwise go unnoticed.

At their core, algorithms follow a set of rules or procedures to solve problems in a systematic way. They have been integral to computer science for decades but now play a transformative role in detecting patterns in data across industries. In the context of data science, algorithms help in tasks such as classification, prediction, and pattern recognition, with applications ranging from personalized marketing to disease detection.

There are two primary types of algorithms used for pattern detection: supervised learning and unsupervised learning. Supervised learning algorithms are trained on labeled data, meaning the outcomes are known during training. These algorithms are learned from the input-output pairs and are used in tasks like predicting stock prices or classifying medical conditions. Unsupervised learning algorithms, on the other hand, work without labeled data and aim to find hidden structures within the data, such as clustering similar customers in marketing analysis.

Neural networks, inspired by the human brain, are particularly powerful for pattern detection in complex data. These networks consist of interconnected layers of nodes and are used in deep learning algorithms to identify intricate patterns in images, speech, and text. Deep learning ability to automatically extract relevant features from raw data has revolutionized fields like computer vision and natural language processing.

While algorithms offer great power, they also raise ethical concerns. Bias in training data can lead to biased outcomes, and the "black box" nature of deep learning can make it difficult to interpret decisions. As algorithms continue to drive decision-making in critical areas like finance, healthcare, and criminal justice, ensuring fairness, transparency, and accountability is essential.

What Are Algorithms?

An algorithm is a set of rules or a procedure for solving a problem in a finite number of steps. While the concept of algorithms dates back centuries (often credited to the Persian mathematician Al-Khwarizmi), today's algorithms are central to the fields of computer science, artificial intelligence, and data analytics. In essence, algorithms automate the process of problem-solving, making it possible to analyze vast amounts of data in ways that would be impossible for humans to do manually.

In the context of data science, algorithms are used to detect patterns, classify information, make predictions, and even learn from new data through processes like machine learning. Algorithms are designed to find structure in data, whether that structure involves recognizing faces in images, predicting stock prices, or detecting fraud in financial transactions.

Supervised and Unsupervised Learning Algorithms

Algorithms used for pattern detection in data science generally fall into two broad categories: supervised learning and unsupervised learning. In supervised learning, algorithms are trained on labeled data. This means that for each data point in the training set, the correct output is already known. The algorithm is learnt from these examples to make predictions on new, unseen data. Supervised learning is used for tasks like classification (e.g., determining whether an email is spam or not) and regression (e.g., predicting the price of a house based on its features). One popular example of a supervised learning algorithm is the decision tree, which makes predictions based on learned decision rules from the data. Unsupervised learning, on the other hand, works with unlabeled data. The goal here is not to make predictions but to find hidden patterns or groupings within the data. Clustering is one of the most common unsupervised learning techniques, where the algorithm groups data points based on their similarities. An example is customer segmentation in marketing, where the goal is to identify different customer groups based on their purchasing behaviors. While supervised learning focuses on prediction, unsupervised learning is more about discovery. Both types of algorithms play a vital role in pattern recognition, but they are applied in different contexts depending on whether the outcome is known in advance or not.

Neural Networks and Deep Learning

Neural networks are a class of algorithms inspired by the human brain's structure and function. They consist of interconnected layers of nodes, or "neurons," that work together to process data and recognize patterns. Each neuron processes inputs, applies a mathematical function, and passes the result to the next layer. Neural networks are particularly powerful because they can model complex relationships and learn from large amounts of data.

Deep learning is a subset of machine learning that uses neural networks with many layers—hence the term "deep." These deep neural networks are capable of handling vast amounts of data and can recognize intricate patterns that simpler algorithms might miss. For example, deep learning algorithms are used in image recognition to identify objects in photos, voice recognition systems to understand spoken language, and natural language processing to analyze and generate human-like text.

One of the key advantages of deep learning is its ability to perform feature extraction automatically. Traditional machine learning algorithms require human experts to manually define the features they want to analyze. In contrast, deep learning algorithms can learn which features are most relevant directly from the data. This has made deep learning especially useful in fields like computer vision, where images contain thousands of potential features that are difficult to define manually.

Reinforcement Learning: Learning by Trial and Error

Another important class of algorithms is reinforcement learning, which differs from supervised and unsupervised learning. Instead of being trained on a fixed dataset, reinforcement learning algorithms learn by interacting with an environment. They receive feedback in the form of rewards or penalties and adjust their behavior to maximize the cumulative reward over time. This trial-and-error approach allows the algorithm to learn strategies that can lead to optimal outcomes.

Reinforcement learning has been successfully applied in various fields, from robotics to game playing. For example, AlphaGo, the program that famously defeated human world champions in the ancient board game Go, used reinforcement learning to master the game. By playing millions of games against itself and learning from the outcomes, AlphaGo discovered strategies that had never been seen before, demonstrating the power of reinforcement learning in complex, strategic environments.

Real-World Applications of Algorithms as Pattern Seekers

Algorithms are transforming industries by enabling the discovery of patterns that were previously invisible to human analysts. In healthcare, machine learning algorithms analyze patient data to detect patterns that can predict the onset of diseases, optimize treatment plans, and even identify potential drug interactions. In finance, algorithms are used to identify fraudulent transactions, forecast market trends, and develop automated trading strategies that react to patterns in market data faster than any human could.

In retail, algorithms power recommend engines that suggest products to customers based on their browsing and purchasing behaviors. These algorithms detect patterns in customer interactions to deliver personalized shopping experiences, which in turn drive sales and customer satisfaction. Netflix and Amazon are well-known examples of companies that leverage recommendation algorithms to keep users engaged and drive revenue.

Algorithms also play a significant role in environmental science, where they are used to model climate change, predict weather patterns, and monitor ecosystems. By analyzing large datasets from satellites and sensors, algorithms can detect changes in temperature, air quality, and biodiversity, providing critical insights for policymakers and environmentalists.

In cybersecurity, algorithms are used for intrusion detection by analyzing network traffic for patterns that indicate potential security threats. Anomaly detection algorithms can identify unusual behavior, such as unauthorized access or suspicious data transfers, allowing organizations to respond to threats in real-time.

The Importance of Interpretability

As algorithms become more complex, particularly with deep learning, one of the growing challenges is interpretability. In some cases, even the developers of an algorithm may not fully understand how it arrived at a specific conclusion, especially in deep learning models with many layers. This lack of transparency, often referred to as the "black box" problem, raises concerns, particularly in fields like healthcare, finance, and criminal justice, where decisions can have significant real-world consequences.

Efforts are being made to improve the interpretability of machine learning models through methods like explainable AI (XAI). These techniques aim to provide insights into how an algorithm makes its decisions, allowing users to understand why certain patterns were recognized and how they led to a particular outcome. As algorithms continue to play a central role in decision-making processes, ensuring their transparency and accountability will be critical.

Challenges and Ethical Considerations

While algorithms offer tremendous potential, they also present significant challenges and ethical concerns. One major issue is bias in algorithms. Since algorithms learn from data, any biases present in the training data can be amplified in the algorithm's predictions. For example, if a facial recognition algorithm is trained predominantly on images of a specific demographic, it may perform poorly when analyzing faces from other demographics. This has led to concerns about fairness and discrimination in AI systems, particularly in applications like hiring, lending, and law enforcement.

Data privacy is another critical concern. Many algorithms rely on personal data to function effectively, raising questions about how that data is collected, stored, and used. As companies and governments increasingly rely on algorithms to drive decisions, it is essential to ensure that individuals' privacy rights are protected.

Additionally, there is the risk of over-reliance on algorithms. While they are powerful tools, algorithms are not infallible. They can make mistakes, particularly when working with incomplete or biased data. It is crucial to maintain a balance between algorithmic decision-making and human oversight to ensure that patterns identified by machines are interpreted correctly and used responsibly.

Conclusion: Algorithms as the Future of Pattern Recognition

Algorithms have revolutionized our ability to detect patterns in vast datasets, allowing us to solve problems and make decisions at a scale and speed that would have been unimaginable just a few decades ago. From supervised learning algorithms that make accurate predictions to unsupervised learning models that uncover hidden structures, and from deep learning networks that process complex data to reinforce learning systems that learn from their own experiences, algorithms are the ultimate pattern seekers.

As we continue to develop more sophisticated algorithms, their applications will expand across industries, from healthcare and finance to environmental science and cybersecurity. However, as we rely more on algorithms to guide critical decisions, it is essential to address challenges related to bias, interpretability, and ethics. Algorithms are powerful tools, but they must be used responsibly to ensure that the patterns they detect are both meaningful and fair.

In the next chapter, we will explore the patterns found in nature, from fractals in plants to the rhythms of ecosystems, and how these natural patterns inspire scientific discoveries and technological advancements.

Chapter 5

Patterns in Nature

Nature presents us with intricate patterns that range from the spirals of galaxies to the delicate veins on a leaf. These natural patterns are not just visually stunning but also hold significant scientific value. They reveal the underlying principles that govern the natural world, from the smallest biological systems to the largest astronomical structures. In science, the study of these patterns has led to breakthroughs in biology, physics, chemistry, and mathematics. This chapter explores prominent patterns found in nature—such as fractals, the Fibonacci sequence, and the golden ratio—and their contributions to both scientific discovery and technological innovation.

Fractals are one of nature's most complex and fascinating patterns. These geometric shapes exhibit self-similarity, meaning that their structure remains consistent regardless of the scale at which they are observed. Whether in the branching of trees, the formation of clouds, or the contours of coastlines, fractals appear repeatedly in natural phenomena. When zooming in on a fractal shape, like a coastline or a fern leaf, you find that the same intricate patterns are repeated infinitely. These fractal structures optimize efficiency, especially in biological systems. For example, river networks that branch into tributaries and streams, much like the bronchi in our lungs, follow fractal geometry to maximize the flow of resources.

The Fibonacci sequence is another mathematical pattern that frequently appears in nature. This series of numbers, in which each number is the sum of the two preceding ones, creates a progression often linked to the golden ratio, approximately 1.618. In nature, you can find Fibonacci sequences in spiral arrangements, such as the seeds in a sunflower or the shells of nautilus sea creatures. These spiral structures, which follow the golden ratio, are not only aesthetically pleasing but also serve a functional purpose. In plants, the arrangement of leaves, called phyllotaxis, often follows Fibonacci patterns to optimize light absorption.

Patterns are also essential in biological systems. At the molecular level, DNA's double helix structure is a repeating pattern that encodes genetic information and ensures the transmission of traits. During an organism's development, patterns arise through the interaction of chemical gradients and cellular interactions. These patterns, such as the stripes on a zebra or the spots on a leopard, are explained through morphogenesis, where genetic and environmental factors shape the growth of organisms.

In physics, patterns are evident in wave phenomena. The interference of sound waves or light waves leads to predictable and often beautiful visual effects, such as the colors in soap bubbles or the diffraction patterns in light. Crystal structures, which form through the ordered arrangement of atoms, are another example of patterns that govern the physical properties of materials, from their strength to conductivity.

These patterns in nature inspire technological innovations. The field of biomimicry, where natural patterns are replicated for human use, has led to inventions like Velcro, modeled after the way burrs stick to fur, and water-repellent surfaces based on the structure of lotus leaves.

In studying these natural patterns, scientists unlock the principles that drive both biological and physical systems. From fractal geometry in nature to the Fibonacci sequence, these patterns help us understand and interact with the world, driving innovations in technology and science.

Fractals: The Geometry of Nature

Fractals are complex geometric shapes that display self-similarity, meaning that their structure remains consistent regardless of the scale at which you observe them. The concept of fractals was formally introduced by mathematician Benoît Mandelbrot in the 1970s, but the phenomenon had long been recognized in the natural world. Fractals can be seen in a variety of natural formations, from the branching of trees to the rugged contours of coastlines. A notable characteristic of fractals is that the closer you examine a fractal structure, the more detail you uncover, and this detail continues to reveal itself infinitely.

In nature, fractals appear in coastlines, where the irregular and jagged shape grows more complex as you zoom in. The length of the coastline, in fact, seems to increase infinitely the closer you inspect it, a direct consequence of its fractal nature. Another striking example is found in plant life, particularly in ferns, where each small leaflet mirrors the shape of the entire leaf, or in Romanesco broccoli, where each bud spirals out in a repeating pattern. Similarly, the branching structure of rivers follows a fractal pattern, where small streams feed into larger tributaries, which in turn connect to the main river. This branching network optimizes the flow of water and nutrients across vast landscapes.

The study of fractals has transformed our understanding of complex systems in nature. It has allowed scientists to model and predict phenomena such as mountain ranges, cloud formations, and even the distribution of galaxies in the universe. In the medical field, fractal geometry is used to analyze the branching patterns of blood vessels and the structure of the lungs, helping doctors understand and treat diseases related to the growth of biological tissues.

The Fibonacci Sequence and the Golden Ratio

The Fibonacci sequence, a series of numbers in which each number is the sum of the two preceding ones, has long fascinated mathematicians and scientists alike. This simple yet profound sequence begins with 0, 1, 2, 3, 5, 8, 13, 21 and continues indefinitely. The ratio between consecutive Fibonacci numbers approaches the golden ratio, approximately 1.618, which has been linked to aesthetically pleasing proportions in art, architecture, and nature.

In the natural world, Fibonacci patterns are everywhere. One of the most famous examples is the spiral arrangement of seeds in a sunflower head. The seeds form spirals that follow the Fibonacci sequence, optimizing space and ensuring that each seed receives sufficient sunlight and nutrients. Similarly, the shells of nautilus sea creature's spiral outward in a logarithmic pattern, following the golden ratio. This pattern is also seen in hurricanes and galaxies, where the swirling spirals conform to the same mathematical principles.

Leaf arrangement, or phyllotaxis, is another natural occurrence of the Fibonacci sequence. Many plants display a spiral pattern in the arrangement of their leaves around a stem, ensuring that each leaf is optimally positioned to capture sunlight. This arrangement, governed by the Fibonacci sequence, allows for the most efficient use of space and resources.

In biology, Fibonacci numbers also appear in the reproductive patterns of certain species. The original example used by Fibonacci to illustrate his sequence involved the breeding patterns of rabbits, which follow a Fibonacci progression. This simple model captures the exponential growth of populations under ideal conditions, though it also applies more broadly to reproductive strategies in nature.

The scientific significance of the Fibonacci sequence and the golden ratio extends beyond botany. In physics and chemistry, these patterns are found in the atomic structures of crystals and the proportions of molecules. Understanding these natural mathematical patterns helps scientists explain how organisms grow, optimize resources, and even how materials form at a microscopic level.

Patterns in Biological Systems

Biological organisms, from the simplest bacteria to the most complex multicellular organisms, exhibit patterns at both macroscopic and microscopic levels. These patterns are often the result of genetic instructions and interactions with the environment.

At the molecular level, one of the most fundamental patterns in biology is the structure of DNA. The double helix of DNA is a highly organized pattern that encodes genetic information. The specific pairing of nucleotide bases—adenine with thymine, and cytosine with guanine—follows strict rules that create a reliable pattern for the replication of genetic material. This molecular pattern is critical for life, as it ensures the accurate transmission of genetic information from one generation to the next.

Another key biological process shaped by patterns is morphogenesis, the development of an organism's shape and structure. Morphogenesis is governed by patterns formed through chemical gradients and cellular interactions. For example, the reaction-diffusion model, developed by mathematician Alan Turing, explains how patterns such as stripes on zebras or spots on leopards emerge during the development of an organism. These patterns arise from the interaction of molecules that inhibit or promote the formation of pigments in the skin, creating the distinct markings seen in many animals.

Ecosystems, too, are governed by patterns, particularly in the interactions between species. The predator-prey relationships that make up food webs are complex, but they form predictable patterns that help maintain ecological balance. By studying these patterns, ecologists can predict how the loss or introduction of a species will affect the overall health of an ecosystem.

Patterns also play a critical role in animal migration. Many species follow migratory routes that are shaped by environmental cues such as the Earth's magnetic field, weather patterns, and the availability of food and water. These migration patterns are essential for the survival of species like birds, fish, and mammals, as they allow them to exploit resources in different regions throughout the year.

Patterns in Physical Systems

In the realm of physics, patterns emerge from the fundamental laws that govern the behavior of matter and energy. Wave patterns, for instance, are a common feature of physical systems. Sound waves, light waves, and even the behavior of particles at the quantum level can be described by mathematical functions that reveal predictable patterns.

The propagation of waves follows patterns that are essential for understanding phenomena like sound and light. For example, interference patterns, created when two waves overlap, lead to effects such as diffraction, which can be observed in the colorful patterns of thin films, like soap bubbles or oil on water. These wave patterns are fundamental to many technologies, from sound engineering to the development of optical devices.

At the atomic level, the arrangement of atoms and molecules in solids forms is highly ordered, repeating patterns known as crystal structures. These patterns determine the physical properties of materials, such as their hardness, melting point, and electrical conductivity. The study of crystallography has led to advances in material science, allowing scientists to design new materials with specific properties based on their atomic patterns.

Quasicrystals, discovered in the 1980s, challenge traditional notions of crystallography. Unlike regular crystals, which have repeating atomic patterns, quasicrystals exhibit ordered but non-repeating patterns. This discovery opened new avenues in material science, as quasicrystals have unique properties, such as low thermal conductivity and high durability, making them useful in various industrial applications.

Patterns in Chemical Systems

Chemical reactions often give rise to patterns through processes such as diffusion and reaction kinetics. A well-known example is the formation of chemical gardens, which occur when metal salts are introduced into a solution of sodium silicate. As the salts react with the silicate, they form intricate plant-like structures. These patterns are the result of a delicate interplay between chemical reactions and physical forces, creating a visually striking representation of how matter organizes itself.

Another fascinating chemical pattern is observed in Belousov-Zhabotinsky reactions, a type of oscillating chemical reaction. In these reactions, the concentrations of different chemicals oscillate over time, creating temporal and spatial patterns such as concentric rings or spirals in a petri dish. These oscillating reactions are valuable for studying non-equilibrium thermodynamics and the behavior of complex systems.

Inspiration for Technological Advancements

Nature's patterns have long inspired technological innovations, particularly in the field of biomimicry. Biomimicry involves studying natural patterns and processes to develop solutions to human challenges. One famous example is Velcro, invented by Swiss engineer George de Mestral after observing how burrs stuck to his dog's fur. Velcro mimics the natural fastening mechanism of burrs, using tiny hooks that latch onto loops, creating a versatile and widely used product.

Another example of biomimicry is the lotus effect. The micro- and nanostructures on the surface of lotus leaves make them extremely water-repellent and self-cleaning. By mimicking this pattern, scientists have developed water-repellent materials that are used in everything from clothing to industrial surfaces.

Architecture and design also draw heavily on natural patterns. Engineers have studied the strength and flexibility of bones, shells, and other biological structures to design buildings and bridges that are both stable and efficient in their use of materials. The field of fractal geometry, for instance, has influenced the design of antennas that can operate over multiple frequencies, improving telecommunications technology.

Mathematical Modeling of Natural Patterns

The mathematical representation of natural patterns allows scientists to simulate and predict complex systems. Chaos theory, for example, is a branch of mathematics that studies how small changes in initial conditions can lead to vastly different outcomes. This concept, often referred to as the "butterfly effect," is crucial in fields like meteorology and economics, where tiny variations in data can have significant consequences.

In computational biology, understanding the patterns of protein folding is essential for drug design and treating diseases caused by misfolded proteins. Mathematical models that describe how proteins fold into specific shapes allow researchers to predict how new drugs will interact with these proteins, speeding up the drug discovery process.

Conclusion: The Symbiosis of Nature and Science

Patterns in nature are far more than aesthetic curiosities; they are the keys to understanding the principles that govern the universe. By studying these patterns, scientists have made significant advancements in fields ranging from medicine and ecology to physics and materials science. The fractal branching of blood vessels informs medical imaging techniques, the efficiency of photosynthesis inspires renewable energy solutions, and the structure of bird wings influences aeronautical engineering.

Nature's patterns serve as both a model and a mentor. They inspire innovation, drive scientific inquiry, and remind us of the interconnectedness of all things. As we continue to explore these natural patterns, we unlock the secrets of the world around us and find sustainable solutions to the challenges of the future.

Chapter 6

Patterns in Business and Society

Patterns are not exclusive to nature; they also shape human behavior, businesses, and societies. From consumer buying habits to stock market fluctuations, patterns help us predict trends, optimize strategies, and make informed decisions. In today's data-driven world, recognizing these patterns is crucial for success across industries. Patterns drive insights that allow businesses to anticipate changes in the market, optimize operations, and respond to societal shifts. One of the most influential areas where patterns emerge is consumer behavior. Companies analyze patterns in customer preferences, purchase history, and demographics to optimize marketing strategies and forecast demand. Retailers like Amazon and Netflix use algorithms to detect patterns in browsing history and previous purchases, offering personal recommendations that enhance the customer experience. This pattern recognition boosts sales and drives customer loyalty. Consumer behavior is also shaped by broader societal trends. Companies that identify shifts in cultural preferences, such as the growing demand for sustainable products, are better positioned to adapt their strategies to meet new market demands.

Supply chain management also benefits from recognizing patterns in production cycles, inventory levels, and delivery times. Efficient supply chains depend on the ability to predict demand and manage resources accordingly. By identifying patterns in historical data, companies can streamline operations, reduce costs, and prevent disruptions. For example, logistics companies use predictive analytics to optimize delivery routes, taking into account patterns in traffic flow and package volumes. This minimizes fuel consumption and improves delivery times, ensuring a more efficient supply chain. Patterns in financial markets are some of the most scrutinized. Traders and analysts rely on recognizing patterns in stock prices, interest rates, and economic indicators to make investment decisions. Algorithmic trading, driven by these patterns, has transformed financial markets, allowing trades to be executed at lightning speed. Investors use technical analysis to detect formations such as trends or chart patterns, which can signal future price movements. Recognizing these patterns helps traders anticipate market behavior and make profitable decisions.

Social media also presents a wealth of patterns, offering insights into public opinion and cultural trends. Platforms like Twitter and Instagram generate vast amounts of data, which businesses and public figures analyze to understand consumer sentiment. By tracking patterns in social media interactions, companies can tailor their messaging to align with the public's interests. Social media patterns also allow for targeted advertising, ensuring that ads reach users whose behaviors and preferences align with the brand. Public sentiment, whether positive or negative, often emerges first through patterns in online discussions, providing companies with real-time feedback. Patterns in urban planning help cities function more efficiently. Data from sensors and connected devices allow planners to identify traffic patterns, optimize public transportation, and manage energy usage. Ride-sharing companies use patterns in demand to deploy vehicles in high-traffic areas, reducing waiting times and enhancing the user experience. Recognizing these patterns ensures that resources are used effectively, contributing to the sustainability of modern cities.

While pattern recognition offers significant advantages, challenges remain, particularly around data privacy and algorithmic bias. Patterns detected in biased data may reinforce social inequalities, while over-reliance on data can overlook the nuances that human judgment provides. As businesses and governments increasingly rely on patterns, it is essential to ensure that they are used ethically and transparently. Patterns are at the heart of decision-making in business and society. By recognizing and leveraging these patterns, organizations can navigate uncertainty, optimize performance, and build better relationships with consumers and citizens.

Consumer Behavior and Market Trends

One of the most influential areas where patterns are found is consumer behavior. Businesses constantly analyze patterns in customer preferences, purchase history, and demographic data to optimize their marketing strategies. By recognizing purchasing trends, companies can forecast demand, tailor products to meet consumer needs, and create personalized shopping experiences. For instance, retail giants like Amazon and Walmart use sophisticated algorithms to analyze customer data, identify patterns, and make recommendations. These recommendation systems detect patterns in browsing behavior and previous purchases to suggest products that align with the customer's interests, driving higher sales and customer satisfaction. Patterns in consumer behavior are not just about personal preferences; they are also influenced by societal trends and cultural shifts. Companies that can identify and respond to broader societal patterns—such as shifts towards sustainability, changing lifestyle preferences, or economic downturns—can adapt their strategies accordingly. The COVID-19 pandemic, for example, led to a surge in online shopping as people shifted to e-commerce platforms. Businesses that quickly recognized this pattern and optimized their online presence thrived during the crisis, while those that lagged behind struggled to keep up with changing consumer demands.

Supply Chain Optimization

Patterns also play a crucial role in supply chain management. Efficient supply chains rely on the ability to predict demand, optimize inventory, and minimize disruptions. Companies use pattern recognition techniques to identify seasonal trends, forecast future demand, and adjust production schedules. By recognizing patterns in customer orders, delivery times, and shipping routes, businesses can streamline their operations, reduce costs, and improve overall efficiency. For instance, companies like FedEx and UPS use predictive analytics to optimize their delivery routes based on historical patterns in traffic and package volumes. This allows them to save time, fuel, and resources while ensuring timely deliveries. In manufacturing, understanding patterns in production cycles helps businesses maintain optimal inventory levels and avoid overproduction or stock shortages. Additionally, the rise of artificial intelligence in logistics has enabled companies to detect and respond to anomalies in real-time, such as disruptions caused by natural disasters or supply chain bottlenecks.

Financial Markets and Economic Patterns

Perhaps one of the most well-known areas where patterns dominate is in financial markets. Investors and analysts have long relied on patterns in stock prices, interest rates, and economic indicators to make informed decisions about buying and selling assets. The use of algorithms in trading, commonly referred to as algorithmic trading, has revolutionized the financial industry. These algorithms analyze historical market data, detect patterns, and execute trades at high speeds, often outperforming human traders. In financial markets, patterns can reveal trends that signal opportunities for investment or risks to avoid. For instance, technical analysis, a popular method used by traders, involves analyzing patterns in stock charts to predict future price movements. By identifying formations like "head and shoulders" or "double bottoms," traders can forecast potential reversals or continuations in price trends. Similarly, machine learning algorithms can sift through massive amounts of financial data, recognizing patterns that indicate bullish or bearish market conditions. Beyond stock trading, patterns in economic data provide insights into the health of economies. Patterns in unemployment rates, inflation, and consumer spending help policymakers and economists make informed decisions. For example, during economic recessions, governments and central banks monitor patterns in economic indicators to adjust monetary policies and implement stimulus packages to stabilize the economy.

Social Media and Public Opinion

In the digital age, patterns in social media data offer a window into public sentiment and social trends. Platforms like Twitter, Facebook, and Instagram generate vast amounts of data, and analyzing this data helps businesses, politicians, and public figures gauge public opinion. By detecting patterns in social media interactions, such as hashtags, mentions, and trending topics, organizations can understand what topics resonate with their audiences, allowing them to tailor their messaging accordingly. Social media platforms also use pattern recognition to target advertisements. By analyzing users' browsing habits, likes, shares, and comments, platforms can serve personalized ads that align with users' interests and preferences. This targeted advertising increases the likelihood of engagement and conversion, making it a powerful tool for businesses seeking to reach specific demographics. Moreover, patterns in social media interactions can serve as early indicators of public sentiment shifts. For instance, a surge in negative comments or the rapid spread of a hashtag may signal a brewing public relations crisis for a company or brand. By recognizing these patterns early, businesses can take proactive steps to address concerns and manage their reputation.

Urban Planning and Human Behavior

Patterns in human behavior extend beyond digital interactions to physical spaces. Urban planners and local governments use data to analyze patterns in traffic flow, public transportation usage, and pedestrian movement to design more efficient cities. By understanding where and when congestion occurs, planners can optimize road layouts, improve public transport schedules, and ensure that cities are designed to meet the needs of their residents.

For example, smart cities leverage data from sensors and connected devices to monitor patterns in energy usage, waste management, and water distribution. This data allows city officials to make informed decisions about resource allocation and infrastructure improvements. In transportation, ride-sharing apps like Uber and Lyft use pattern recognition to predict peak demand times and locations, optimizing their fleet distribution to reduce wait times for users.

Beyond infrastructure, patterns in human movement and social behavior also influence the development of public spaces. Cities that understand the patterns of how people use parks, plazas, and recreational areas can create more inviting and functional environments. Data-driven urban planning ensures that resources are allocated efficiently, contributing to sustainable and livable cities.

Challenges in Pattern Recognition in Society

While pattern recognition offers significant advantages in business and society, it also presents challenges. One of the main concerns is the potential for bias in algorithms and data analysis. If the data used to detect patterns is biased or incomplete, the resulting patterns may reinforce existing inequalities or lead to unfair outcomes. For example, biased algorithms in hiring or lending practices can perpetuate discrimination based on race, gender, or socioeconomic status.

Privacy is another critical concern in the era of data-driven decision-making. As companies and governments increasingly rely on data to detect patterns, individuals' personal information is often collected and analyzed. This raises ethical questions about how data is used, who has access to it, and how individuals' privacy can be protected in a world where data is currency.

Finally, while pattern recognition can improve efficiency and decision-making, it is essential to strike a balance between data-driven approaches and human intuition. Over-reliance on algorithms can lead to automated decisions that lack the nuance and context that human judgment provides. Ensuring that patterns are interpreted within the broader context of human experience is crucial for making decisions that are both accurate and ethical.

Conclusion: The Power of Patterns in Shaping Business and Society

Patterns are at the heart of decision-making in business and society. Whether through consumer behavior, financial markets, social media trends, or urban planning, the ability to recognize and respond to patterns allows organizations to optimize their operations, predict future trends, and engage more effectively with their customers and citizens. As data continues to drive the modern world, the importance of identifying and understanding patterns will only grow, helping to shape the future of business and society in profound ways.

Chapter 7

The Role of Patterns in Technology

Technology, in many ways, is built on the ability to recognize and exploit patterns. Whether it's the algorithms powering machine learning, the codes enabling encryption, or the designs that streamline software development, patterns lie at the heart of technological advancement. This capacity to detect and harness these patterns has transformed industries, driven innovation, and reshaped the way we interact with the world. From artificial intelligence (AI) to cybersecurity and software engineering, recognizing patterns has become the foundation for creating more efficient, secure, and intelligent systems.

At its core, technology thrives on pattern recognition because patterns allow for automation, prediction, and problem-solving at a scale that human minds alone could not achieve. Computers and software systems excel in detecting patterns in massive datasets, making decisions, and even learning new patterns over time. This ability to find structure in seemingly unstructured data has revolutionized industries such as healthcare, finance, and education, allowing organizations to make data-driven decisions with greater speed and accuracy.

One of the most significant examples of pattern recognition in technology is found in artificial intelligence (AI) and machine learning. AI systems are designed to simulate human intelligence by recognizing patterns in data and using these patterns to make decisions or predictions. Machine learning, a subset of AI, involves training algorithms to detect patterns in data without explicit programming for each task. For instance, image recognition systems use machine learning algorithms to analyze patterns in pixels to identify objects, people, or scenes. These algorithms can distinguish between a cat and a dog based on the patterns learned from millions of images during training. Similarly, voice assistants like Siri and Alexa rely on speech pattern recognition to understand and respond to user commands.

A more advanced form of machine learning, known as deep learning, takes pattern recognition to new heights by using artificial neural networks that mimic the way the human brain processes information. These networks consist of multiple layers of nodes, where each layer recognizes increasingly abstract patterns. Deep learning is behind major advancements in natural language processing (NLP), autonomous vehicles, and facial recognition technology. For example, autonomous vehicles rely on deep learning algorithms to recognize patterns in the environment, such as road signs, pedestrians, and other vehicles, allowing them to navigate complex situations without human intervention.

Beyond AI, patterns play a crucial role in cybersecurity. The ability to detect abnormal patterns in network traffic or user behavior is key to preventing cyberattacks. Cybersecurity systems use pattern recognition to identify potential threats based on deviations from normal activity. For example, an unusual login from an unfamiliar location or a spike in data transfer could indicate a security breach. Systems that monitor and protect against such anomalies are constantly updated to recognize new patterns of attack, helping to secure sensitive information and prevent data breaches. Encryption, another vital aspect of cybersecurity, also relies on patterns—specifically, the creation of codes that transform readable data into an unreadable format. Encryption algorithms create patterns that can only be decoded by those with the correct key, ensuring the secure transmission of information across networks.

In software development, recognizing and applying patterns is essential for building scalable and efficient applications. Software developers use design patterns—reusable solutions to common coding challenges—to streamline the development process. These patterns provide standardized approaches to handling repetitive tasks, reducing the complexity of software systems. For instance, the Model-View-Controller (MVC) design pattern is widely used in web development to separate concerns and organize code more effectively. The MVC pattern splits an application into three components: the model, which handles data; the view, which manages the user interface; and the controller, which connects the two. By using patterns like MVC, developers can improve code readability, facilitate team collaboration, and speed up the development process.

The importance of pattern recognition extends beyond AI, cybersecurity, and software engineering into broader technological advancements. In data science, identifying meaningful patterns within massive datasets allows businesses and researchers to uncover trends, predict outcomes, and make better decisions. For instance, predictive analytics relies on recognizing historical patterns to forecast future behavior, such as predicting customer churn or financial market trends. Similarly, anomaly detection uses pattern recognition to spot outliers in data, which could signal fraud, equipment failure, or even medical conditions in healthcare diagnostics.

As technology continues to evolve, the role of pattern recognition will only become more crucial. From AI-driven innovations to the secure management of digital information, recognizing and leveraging patterns enables us to build smarter, more efficient systems that can solve increasingly complex problems. The future of technology lies in our ability to understand and exploit the patterns that govern the digital world.

Patterns in Artificial Intelligence and Machine Learning

Artificial Intelligence (AI) relies heavily on pattern recognition. In machine learning, a subset of AI, algorithms are trained to detect patterns in data, allowing them to make predictions, classify information, or identify relationships that would be impossible for humans to spot. These algorithms, once trained, can analyze vast amounts of data at high speed, uncovering insights that are otherwise hidden in the noise.

Supervised learning, where models are trained on labeled data, exemplifies how AI uses patterns to make accurate predictions. For instance, an AI system trained to recognize images of cats learns patterns related to fur texture, shape, and color. Once these patterns are internalized, the AI can quickly identify new images of cats it has never seen before. Similarly, unsupervised learning identifies patterns in unlabeled data, such as customer behavior or product recommendations, clustering data into meaningful groups.

Deep learning, a more advanced subset of machine learning, goes further by using neural networks with multiple layers. These networks can recognize even more complex patterns, such as human speech, handwriting, or facial expressions. The ability of deep learning systems to learn hierarchical patterns has led to breakthroughs in fields like natural language processing, image recognition, and autonomous vehicles.

Cybersecurity and Encryption

Patterns are also at the core of cybersecurity, where the identification of suspicious patterns in network traffic or data access can prevent potential breaches. Anomalies in data, such as unusual login times or sudden spikes in network activity, often indicate a security threat. Intrusion detection systems (IDS) rely on recognizing these abnormal patterns to flag potential cyberattacks.

Encryption, another cornerstone of cybersecurity, also involves the creation and recognition of patterns. Encryption algorithms transform data into unreadable formats, making it accessible only to those with the decryption key. In many encryption schemes, patterns in the encrypted data are deliberately obscured to prevent adversaries from recognizing patterns and reverse-engineering the original data. By understanding and manipulating patterns in encryption algorithms, cybersecurity professionals can protect sensitive information and ensure data privacy.

Patterns in Software Development

In software development, patterns are critical to creating scalable and efficient systems. Developers rely on design patterns—reusable solutions to common problems in software design—to streamline the development process. These patterns provide a blueprint for solving issues related to structure, behavior, or data management in software projects. The use of design patterns enables developers to write code that is both efficient and maintainable.

One well-known example of a design pattern is the "Model-View-Controller" (MVC) pattern, which separates an application into three interconnected components: the model (data), the view (user interface), and the controller (logic). By structuring applications in this way, developers can work on different parts of the software simultaneously, improving productivity and reducing complexity. Design patterns like this one are invaluable in large-scale software development, where maintaining clarity and organization is essential.

Another important pattern in software development is the use of algorithms to optimize performance. Algorithms are designed to solve specific computational problems, and by recognizing patterns in the type of problem, developers can select the most appropriate algorithm. For example, sorting algorithms like quicksort or merge sort are used to organize data efficiently based on its structure. Recognizing patterns in the data allows developers to choose the optimal algorithm, ensuring faster and more efficient performance.

Pattern Recognition in Data Science

Data science is driven by the need to detect meaningful patterns in vast datasets. As businesses, governments, and researchers collect more data than ever before, the ability to identify patterns has become crucial for making informed decisions. Whether it's finding trends in customer behavior, detecting fraud in financial transactions, or forecasting weather patterns, data scientists rely on algorithms that can sift through the data and reveal hidden patterns.

One of the most common applications of pattern recognition in data science is in predictive analytics. Businesses use predictive analytics to analyze historical data and make informed decisions about future outcomes. By recognizing patterns in past sales data, for example, a company can predict future demand and adjust its inventory accordingly. Similarly, in healthcare, pattern recognition algorithms help identify patients who are at risk of developing certain diseases, allowing for early intervention and treatment.

Pattern recognition is also vital in anomaly detection, where algorithms identify outliers or unusual patterns in data. In industries like finance, these patterns can indicate fraud or errors, enabling companies to take preventive action before the damage is done.

Patterns in Human-Computer Interaction

The way humans interact with technology also involves recognizing patterns. In human-computer interaction (HCI), designers create user interfaces based on established patterns of behavior. For example, most websites follow similar patterns in terms of layout and navigation, allowing users to interact with new sites more easily because they recognize familiar patterns from previous experiences. This consistency in design patterns improves usability and reduces the cognitive load on users.

Gesture recognition is another area where patterns in human behavior are leveraged. Modern devices like smartphones and gaming consoles use sensors to detect patterns in hand movements, allowing users to interact with the device without physical input. For example, swiping left or right on a touchscreen is a recognized pattern of interaction that users have come to expect. By understanding these behavioral patterns, developers can create more intuitive and user-friendly systems.

Challenges and Future Directions

While pattern recognition has transformed technology, it also presents challenges. One of the biggest concerns is the potential for bias in algorithms. If an algorithm is trained on biased data, it may learn patterns that reflect or reinforce existing inequalities. For example, facial recognition algorithms have been criticized for exhibiting racial and gender biases, as they often perform better on data that resembles the individuals they were trained on. Addressing these biases is crucial as pattern recognition continues to be integrated into everyday technologies.

Another challenge is ensuring transparency in how algorithms detect and use patterns. Deep learning models, in particular, are often referred to as "black boxes" because their internal processes are difficult to interpret. As these models are increasingly used in critical areas like healthcare and criminal justice, there is a growing need for explainable AI—systems that can provide insight into how decisions are made.

Looking to the future, the role of patterns in technology will only grow. As technologies like AI, machine learning, and quantum computing continue to advance, recognizing and harnessing patterns will be key to solving complex problems and driving innovation across industries.

Conclusion: Patterns as the Foundation of Technological Progress

Patterns are the building blocks of technological innovation. From machine learning and cybersecurity to software development and data science, the ability to recognize and leverage patterns enables more efficient, secure, and intelligent systems. As we continue to push the boundaries of technology, pattern recognition will remain at the forefront, guiding the development of smarter and more capable technologies.

Chapter 8

Patterns In Innovation and Creativity

Innovation and creativity, often perceived as sudden bursts of inspiration, are in fact deeply rooted in the recognition and manipulation of patterns. While the popular image of the lone genius suggests that breakthroughs happen in isolation, the reality is more structured. Innovation follows a predictable process, one shaped by a combination of existing knowledge, past experiences, and even failures. It is the ability to identify patterns, connect seemingly unrelated ideas, and apply these insights in novel ways that forms the foundation of creative problem-solving.

In science, for example, many groundbreaking discoveries have emerged when existing patterns from one field are applied to solve problems in another. Biomimicry, which takes inspiration from nature's patterns, has led to numerous technological innovations. Examples include Velcro, inspired by the hooks of burrs clinging to animal fur, and the development of efficient aerodynamic designs based on the wings of birds. These innovations demonstrate how recognizing patterns in natural processes can lead to technological advancements that push industries forward.

In business, innovation frequently stems from spotting market trends and consumer behavior patterns before competitors do. Companies that can identify emerging patterns in consumer needs or preferences are able to adapt their strategies, create new products, and seize opportunities. This pattern-based foresight is key to staying ahead in rapidly changing industries.

The same is true in the arts, where creativity often emerges through the recognition and reinterpretation of visual, auditory, or narrative patterns. Artists, composers, and writers use established patterns—whether in form, rhythm, or storytelling—as frameworks to create something new. By building on and sometimes breaking away from these established patterns, they are able to produce innovative works that push the boundaries of their respective fields.

The Creative Process: Finding Patterns in Chaos

Creativity, despite its seemingly chaotic nature, often follows patterns of thinking that lead to new ideas. One of the most well-known models of the creative process, the "Four Stages of Creativity," provides a framework that illustrates how pattern recognition underlies creative breakthroughs. These four stages—preparation, incubation, illumination, and verification—are driven by the brain's ability to absorb, process, and connect patterns in novel ways.

In the preparation stage, the individual gathers information and immerses themselves in a problem or area of interest. This is where pattern recognition begins, as the person familiarizes themselves with existing knowledge, trends, and challenges. During incubation, the mind subconsciously processes the information gathered, often finding connections between previously unlinked ideas. This period of unconscious thought allows the brain to make sense of complex patterns. The moment of illumination or insight occurs when the mind suddenly forms a new pattern, connecting disparate pieces of information in a way that sparks a creative breakthrough. Finally, in the verification stage, the idea is tested, refined, and evaluated for practicality.

This process of recognizing patterns and connecting them in new ways is at the heart of innovation. Many groundbreaking ideas, from scientific discoveries to artistic masterpieces, result from individuals seeing patterns where others did not. The ability to step back, see the bigger picture, and link seemingly unrelated concepts is essential to creativity.

Innovation in Science and Technology: Applying Old Patterns to New Problems

In science and technology, innovation often emerges when existing patterns are applied to new contexts. The concept of "transferable patterns" is crucial to innovation—discovering solutions in one field and applying them to solve problems in another. For example, biomimicry, where nature's patterns inspire technological solutions, has led to innovations such as Velcro (inspired by the hooks of burrs) and aerodynamic designs based on bird wings.

Similarly, many scientific breakthroughs are the result of recognizing patterns across disciplines. For instance, DNA's double-helix structure, one of the most significant discoveries in biology, was identified because scientists recognized a familiar pattern in molecular structures. In physics, patterns like wave-particle duality helped lay the foundation for quantum mechanics, transforming how we understand the nature of matter and energy. Scientists who can identify patterns across different domains often unlock new insights and develop groundbreaking technologies.

In today's world, data science and artificial intelligence are driving innovation by enabling computers to recognize patterns in vast datasets. AI models trained on these patterns are revolutionizing industries, from healthcare to autonomous vehicles. For instance, machine learning algorithms that detect patterns in medical images have made it possible to diagnose diseases like cancer with unprecedented accuracy, paving the way for more personalized treatments. Similarly, pattern recognition in financial data helps identify market trends, allowing businesses and investors to make data-driven decisions.

Business Innovation: Spotting Market Patterns and Trends

In the business world, innovation is often tied to the ability to spot market trends and consumer behavior patterns. Companies that can identify emerging patterns before their competitors are better positioned to adapt to changes, create new products, and meet evolving customer needs. For example, the rise of digital streaming services like Netflix and Spotify was driven by recognizing the pattern of declining interest in physical media and the growing demand for on-demand, personalized content.

Businesses use tools like predictive analytics and market research to analyze consumer data and detect patterns that indicate future trends. By studying purchasing habits, social media activity, and economic indicators, companies can anticipate what customers will want next. This ability to forecast demand enables businesses to innovate by developing new products or services that align with emerging patterns in consumer behavior.

Companies that succeed in innovation are often those that can disrupt existing industries by recognizing patterns others have missed. For instance, the success of Uber and Lyft came from identifying a pattern in urban mobility—a gap between traditional taxi services and the need for more flexible, technology-driven transportation solutions. By using ride-sharing technology, these companies transformed the transportation industry and set the stage for further innovations like autonomous vehicles.

Art and Creativity: Patterns in Expression

Artistic creativity also relies on recognizing and manipulating patterns, whether through visual composition, rhythm in music, or storytelling in literature. In visual arts, patterns play a critical role in the composition of paintings, sculptures, and digital art. Artists use patterns of color, shape, and texture to create balance, rhythm, and harmony within a piece. Similarly, architects design buildings based on repeating patterns and geometric principles that both functionally and aesthetically shape spaces.

Music is another realm where patterns are central to creativity. Composers create patterns of notes, rhythms, and harmonies to evoke emotions and tell stories. These musical patterns form the foundation of melody, harmony, and rhythm, which composers manipulate to create new works. In literature, writers rely on patterns in language, narrative structure, and character development to engage readers and convey meaning.

Pattern recognition in art and creativity is not limited to replicating existing forms. Often, the most innovative artists are those who break from traditional patterns, challenging conventions and introducing new ways of seeing and interpreting the world. Abstract art, for instance, reimagines traditional forms by emphasizing shapes and colors over realistic representation, creating new visual patterns that push the boundaries of artistic expression.

The Role of Failure in Innovation: Learning from Patterns

Failure, too, plays a vital role in the innovation process, as it helps individuals and organizations recognize patterns in what doesn't work. By analyzing failed attempts, innovators can identify flaws in their strategies, processes, or designs, and use this knowledge to improve future efforts. Failure often reveals important patterns—whether in market response, technical challenges, or design limitations—that might otherwise be overlooked.

Many successful entrepreneurs and inventors emphasize the importance of learning from failure, seeing it not as a setback but as an opportunity to identify patterns of mistakes and pivot towards more effective solutions. This iterative process of trial and error, where patterns of failure lead to new insights, is key to refining creative ideas and driving innovation forward.

Conclusion: Patterns as the Blueprint for Innovation

Patterns are at the core of both innovation and creativity, whether in art, science, business, or technology. By recognizing patterns, individuals can connect ideas, generate new solutions, and bring about breakthroughs that drive progress. From biomimicry in engineering to predictive analytics in business, the ability to detect, analyze, and apply patterns is central to the creative process. While creativity may seem like an abstract or spontaneous act, it is often rooted in a deep understanding of the patterns that shape our world. As we continue to innovate, recognizing these patterns will remain essential to unlocking the full potential of human creativity and ingenuity.

Chapter 9

The Future of Pattern Recognition

As we navigate the complexities of the digital age, the future of pattern recognition emerges as a pivotal force shaping innovation across numerous fields. The ability to detect, analyze, and apply patterns has already transformed industries such as healthcare, finance, and technology. As advancements continue, the scope of pattern recognition will only expand, offering new opportunities for growth and discovery. At the forefront of this evolution is artificial intelligence (AI). As computational power increases and algorithms become more sophisticated, machines will be better equipped to recognize patterns within complex datasets. The rise of explainable AI (XAI) seeks to enhance transparency in AI decision-making processes, allowing users to understand how conclusions are drawn. This is particularly important in sectors like healthcare, where trust in AI systems can significantly impact patient outcomes. Another area of growth is the integration of neuromyotonic AI, which combines neural networks with symbolic reasoning. This approach enables machines to recognize patterns while also applying logical reasoning to understand context, leading to systems that think more like humans. This evolution could enhance natural language processing and improve how virtual assistants interact with users. The applications of pattern recognition are set to expand significantly across various sectors. In healthcare, for instance, the capacity to analyze patient data will facilitate early disease detection and personalized treatment plans. Predictive analytics can help identify patients at risk for conditions such as diabetes or heart disease, enabling timely interventions that improve health outcomes. In finance, pattern recognition will enhance fraud detection and risk assessment. Machine learning algorithms will analyze transaction patterns to spot anomalies indicative of fraudulent activity. This proactive approach to cybersecurity will protect consumers and organizations alike. Smart cities will also benefit from advancements in pattern recognition. By analyzing data from IoT devices, city planners can identify patterns in traffic and energy consumption, leading to improved resource allocation and enhanced urban living. In education, pattern recognition can transform personalized learning experiences. By analyzing student data, educators can tailor instructional strategies to meet individual needs, promoting engagement and improving outcomes. The future of pattern recognition is bright and filled with possibilities. As technology continues to evolve, our ability to harness these patterns will remain a cornerstone of innovation, shaping the way we live, work, and interact with the world.

Advancements in Artificial Intelligence

At the forefront of the future of pattern recognition is the evolution of artificial intelligence (AI) and machine learning. As computational power increases and algorithms become more sophisticated, the ability of machines to recognize patterns in complex datasets will grow exponentially. This advancement is critical, as the volume of data generated worldwide is projected to increase dramatically, creating a need for more efficient and effective pattern recognition systems. One significant area of development is the rise of explainable AI (XAI). Traditional machine learning models, particularly deep learning systems, often operate as "black boxes," where the decision-making process is opaque and difficult to interpret. XAI seeks to make AI more transparent, allowing users to understand the reasoning behind the outcomes produced by algorithms. This is particularly important in sectors such as healthcare and finance, where the stakes are high, and understanding the rationale behind decisions is crucial for trust and accountability. For example, in medical diagnostics, an AI system that identifies patterns in imaging data to diagnose diseases must provide explanations for its findings. A physician needs to understand why the system flagged a particular image as indicative of a disease to make informed treatment decisions. By fostering transparency, XAI can enhance user confidence and ensure that pattern recognition systems are used responsibly and effectively. Another promising direction in AI is the integration of neurosymbolic AI, which combines neural networks with symbolic reasoning. This hybrid approach enables machines to recognize patterns while applying logical reasoning to understand context. By bridging the gap between statistical pattern recognition and human-like reasoning, neuromyotonic AI has the potential to create systems that are more intelligent and capable of handling complex tasks that require nuanced understanding. For instance, in natural language processing, this approach could lead to advancements in conversational AI, allowing virtual assistants to grasp context and intent more effectively.

Expanding Applications Across Industries

The applications of pattern recognition are poised to expand significantly across multiple sectors. In healthcare, the ability to recognize patterns in patient data can lead to early detection of diseases and personalized treatment plans. As electronic health records (EHRs) continue to proliferate, data scientists and healthcare providers can analyze historical patient data to identify patterns indicative of health risks. Machine learning models that detect anomalies in health metrics can alert clinicians to potential issues before they escalate, improving patient outcomes and reducing healthcare costs. For example, predictive analytics in healthcare can help identify patients at high risk for conditions such as diabetes or heart disease based on historical patterns in their medical records, lifestyle, and genetic information. By intervening early, healthcare providers can implement preventive measures, leading to better health outcomes for patients and more efficient use of healthcare resources. In finance, the future of pattern recognition will involve developing more robust systems for fraud detection and risk assessment. Financial institutions are increasingly leveraging machine learning algorithms to analyze transaction patterns and identify anomalies that may indicate fraudulent activity. As cybercriminals continuously adapt their tactics, the ability to recognize evolving patterns in financial data will be crucial for protecting both consumers and organizations.

Moreover, pattern recognition will play a key role in algorithmic trading, where sophisticated algorithms analyze market data to identify patterns that signal investment opportunities. By recognizing trends in stock prices, trading volumes, and economic indicators, financial institutions can make data-driven decisions that maximize returns while minimizing risks. The concept of smart cities exemplifies how pattern recognition can optimize urban living. As cities become more connected through the Internet of Things (IoT), vast amounts of data will be generated from sensors monitoring traffic, energy usage, and public transportation. By analyzing this data, city planners can identify patterns that inform decisions about resource allocation, traffic management, and environmental sustainability. For instance, analyzing traffic patterns in real-time can help adjust traffic signals to minimize congestion and improve commute times. Similarly, recognizing patterns in energy consumption can inform strategies for reducing energy waste and enhancing the efficiency of public services. In the realm of education, pattern recognition can transform personalized learning experiences. By analyzing students' learning patterns, educators can identify areas where individuals may struggle and tailor instructional strategies accordingly. Adaptive learning technologies utilize pattern recognition to adjust content delivery based on students' progress, ensuring that learning experiences are customized to meet their unique needs.

The Role of Data and Technology in Enhancing Pattern Recognition

The advancement of data analytics and computational technologies will continue to enhance pattern recognition capabilities across various fields. As big data technologies evolve, they will allow organizations to process and analyze larger datasets more efficiently. Machine learning frameworks and data visualization tools will enable researchers and practitioners to extract insights from complex data structures and identify patterns that may not be apparent through traditional analysis methods. Cloud computing also plays a critical role in the future of pattern recognition. By providing scalable resources for data storage and processing, cloud platforms enable organizations to harness the power of pattern recognition without the constraints of physical infrastructure. This scalability allows for real-time data analysis, making it easier to detect patterns as they emerge and respond proactively. In addition, advancements in edge computing will further enhance the ability to recognize patterns in real-time. By processing data closer to its source—such as sensors in smart devices—edge computing reduces latency and bandwidth usage, allowing for quicker insights and decision-making. This is particularly important in applications like autonomous vehicles, where real-time pattern recognition is crucial for navigating complex environments safely.

Human Creativity and Intuition in Pattern Recognition

While technology continues to advance, the human element in pattern recognition remains vital. Human creativity, intuition, and empathy play irreplaceable roles in understanding context, nuance, and emotional intelligence. The best outcomes will arise from collaborative efforts between humans and machines, leveraging the strengths of both. As we look toward the future, interdisciplinary collaboration will be essential. Researchers, developers, and data scientists must work together to ensure that pattern recognition technologies are developed and deployed in ways that maximize their effectiveness and utility. Engaging in public discourse about the societal impacts of these technologies will help shape policies that prioritize positive outcomes while fostering innovation. Moreover, as pattern recognition technology becomes more embedded in daily life, the public must be educated about its implications. Understanding how data is collected, analyzed, and used will empower individuals to make informed choices about their digital lives and advocate for their rights.

The Role of Pattern Recognition in Driving Innovation

Pattern recognition is fundamentally linked to innovation, driving new ideas and solutions across various domains. By recognizing patterns, individuals can generate novel connections that lead to breakthroughs. This is particularly important in creative fields such as art, design, and entertainment, where the ability to identify patterns in audience preferences can inspire new forms of expression. For example, filmmakers and game developers increasingly analyze audience data to identify trends in storytelling and character development. By understanding the patterns that resonate with viewers and players, creators can craft more engaging narratives that appeal to their target audiences. This data-driven approach to creativity can lead to innovative works that push the boundaries of traditional storytelling. In the business world, companies that successfully leverage pattern recognition to innovate are more likely to thrive. By identifying market trends and consumer preferences, organizations can develop products and services that align with emerging demands. The rise of sustainable consumer products is a response to a pattern of increasing environmental awareness among consumers. Companies that recognize this trend and adapt their offerings are better positioned to succeed in a competitive marketplace.

Looking Ahead: The Future Landscape of Pattern Recognition

As we move toward a future where pattern recognition becomes increasingly integrated into our daily lives, the landscape will be shaped by continual advancements in technology and data analysis. New algorithms will emerge, enhancing our ability to identify subtle and complex patterns. Moreover, the growth of quantum computing has the potential to revolutionize data processing capabilities, allowing for the analysis of patterns in data sets that are currently too large or complex for classical computing methods. The future of pattern recognition is bright and filled with possibilities that extend across diverse fields. As technology continues to evolve, the ability to recognize and apply patterns will remain a cornerstone of innovation. By advancing AI capabilities, expanding applications, and embracing the human element in pattern recognition, we can harness the full potential of this powerful tool. The journey ahead will be one of discovery, collaboration, and responsible stewardship, ensuring that the benefits of pattern recognition are realized for all.

Chapter 10

Connecting the Dots-Embracing the Patterns of Life

As we conclude our exploration of patterns, it becomes evident that they are not merely abstract concepts confined to the realms of mathematics and science. Instead, patterns are the very threads that weave together our understanding of the world. From the intricate designs found in nature to the algorithms driving technological innovations, patterns serve as fundamental building blocks that help us make sense of complex systems, guide our decision-making, and inspire creativity. They are the lenses through which we interpret our experiences and the tools we use to navigate the intricacies of life. Throughout this book, we have journeyed through various domains, uncovering the significance of patterns in nature, business, technology, and human creativity. In nature, we observed how the Fibonacci sequence manifests in the arrangements of leaves, the spirals of shells, and the branching of trees, demonstrating that mathematics is woven into the fabric of life itself. These natural patterns not only inform scientists and mathematicians but also inspire artists and designers, showing us that the beauty of nature is inherently tied to its structure and form. In the realm of business, we discovered how recognizing patterns in consumer behavior can lead to innovative strategies and successful products. Companies that harness these insights can anticipate market trends, adapt to changing consumer preferences, and foster stronger relationships with their customers. This understanding highlights the importance of data analytics and market research, where businesses leverage pattern recognition to drive growth and stay competitive. As we explored technology, we delved into how advancements in artificial intelligence and machine learning enhance our ability to detect and analyze patterns within vast datasets. These technologies have the potential to revolutionize industries, from healthcare—where they can help identify diseases early—to finance, where they can detect fraudulent activities. The implications of pattern recognition in technology extend far beyond efficiency; they hold the promise of transforming lives by providing insights that lead to better decision-making and improved outcomes. Moreover, we reflected on the role of patterns in human creativity, emphasizing that artists, writers, and musicians often draw from existing patterns to innovate and express themselves. Recognizing these patterns allows them to build on previous works, blend different styles, and create something entirely new. This interplay between recognition and innovation is what drives artistic expression and contributes to cultural evolution. As we reflect on this journey, it's essential to appreciate the interconnectivity of these patterns and the holistic view they provide. Patterns are not isolated phenomena; they exist in a complex web of relationships that shape our understanding of the world. By recognizing these connections, we can approach problems with a more integrated mindset, fostering collaboration across disciplines and encouraging the exchange of ideas. Ultimately, the exploration of patterns is not just about identifying structures or trends; it's about fostering a deeper understanding of the world around us. As we continue to seek out and embrace the patterns in our lives, we open ourselves to a wealth of knowledge and creativity, equipping us to navigate the complexities of the modern world with confidence and insight.

The Interconnectedness of Patterns

One of the most striking insights from our exploration is the interconnectedness of patterns across different fields. For instance, the Fibonacci sequence is not only a mathematical curiosity but also a principle that appears in biology, art, and architecture. This sequence manifests in the arrangement of leaves, the branching of trees, and the spirals of shells, illustrating how mathematical patterns govern natural forms. Similarly, fractals demonstrate how complex forms can arise from simple rules, showcasing a shared language across natural phenomena, technology, and design. The self-similar structures of coastlines, mountain ranges, and clouds illustrate how intricate designs emerge from fundamental principles. This interconnectedness serves as a reminder that the boundaries we often draw between disciplines are not as rigid as they may seem. Instead, they are porous, allowing for the cross-pollination of ideas and methods. The most significant innovations often arise at the intersection of different fields, where diverse perspectives and patterns converge to create something new and transformative. For example, the integration of biology and technology has given rise to bioinformatics, a field that utilizes computational techniques to analyze biological data. By recognizing the patterns within genetic sequences, researchers can make breakthroughs in medicine and genetics, ultimately improving health outcomes. In the arts, recognizing patterns in different cultural expressions can inspire new forms of creativity. Artists often draw inspiration from various styles, techniques, and mediums, weaving them together to create innovative works. This synthesis of ideas exemplifies how the recognition of patterns across disciplines can lead to fresh perspectives and artistic breakthroughs.

Embracing the Future of Patterns

As we look to the future, the potential for pattern recognition to drive progress is immense. With advancements in artificial intelligence and machine learning, our ability to analyze and interpret vast amounts of data will continue to grow. This evolution will enable us to uncover hidden patterns that can inform decision-making in real time, from healthcare diagnostics to climate change modeling. For instance, in the field of climate science, pattern recognition can analyze historical climate data to predict future trends and impacts. Understanding the patterns of temperature fluctuations, precipitation levels, and extreme weather events can inform policymakers and help communities prepare for and mitigate the effects of climate change. In healthcare, pattern recognition will revolutionize diagnostics and treatment. Advanced algorithms can analyze patient data, identifying patterns that indicate potential health risks. This proactive approach can lead to early intervention, personalized treatment plans, and improved health outcomes. As we harness the power of patterns, the potential for better healthcare delivery becomes increasingly tangible. However, embracing this future also calls for a commitment to continuous learning and adaptation. As our tools and technologies evolve, so too must our approaches to understanding and utilizing patterns. This includes fostering interdisciplinary collaboration, encouraging creative thinking, and being open to new ideas that challenge existing paradigms. For example, fostering partnerships between data scientists, medical professionals, and engineers can lead to innovative solutions that leverage pattern recognition for better healthcare delivery. This collaboration can enhance our ability to analyze complex patient data and develop targeted interventions.

The Role of Human Intuition

While technology will undoubtedly enhance our capacity for pattern recognition, it is crucial to remember the indispensable role of human intuition and creativity. Patterns provide a framework for understanding, but it is human insight that brings context and meaning to these patterns. As we integrate advanced technologies into our lives, maintaining a balance between machine-driven analysis and human judgment will be vital. Encouraging curiosity, nurturing creativity, and fostering a culture of exploration will enable us to harness the full potential of patterns. By cultivating environments that support innovative thinking and interdisciplinary collaboration, we can unlock new insights and drive meaningful change. In creative fields such as art and literature, human intuition plays a crucial role in interpreting and reshaping patterns.

Artists often experiment with existing patterns, breaking conventions to create new forms of expression. This creative exploration can lead to groundbreaking works that challenge perceptions and provoke thought. In business, leaders who recognize and respond to patterns in consumer behavior can develop strategies that resonate with their audience. By understanding the underlying motivations and preferences of customers, businesses can create products and services that meet evolving demands.

A Call to Action

As we conclude this exploration of patterns, I invite you to embrace the power of patterns in your own life and work. Whether you are a scientist, an artist, a business leader, or simply a curious individual, recognizing and leveraging patterns can lead to transformative insights and solutions. Consider the patterns that surround you in your daily experiences, the natural world, your work, and your relationships. How can you draw connections between seemingly disparate elements? How can you apply the insights gained from these patterns to drive innovation, solve problems, or inspire others? In a world increasingly driven by data and complexity, the ability to recognize, analyze, and apply patterns will be an invaluable skill. It is a skill that transcends disciplines, uniting the realms of science, art, technology, and human experience. By cultivating this skill, we can navigate the complexities of our world with greater clarity, creativity, and purpose.

The Ongoing Journey of Discovery

The exploration of patterns is not merely an academic exercise; it is an ongoing journey that invites curiosity, creativity, and collaboration. As we continue to seek out patterns in our lives, we open ourselves to a world of possibilities, ready to embrace the challenges and opportunities that lie ahead. By recognizing patterns in our daily interactions, we can enhance our relationships and foster connections that contribute to personal growth and community well-being. Whether it's identifying patterns in communication styles, understanding shared experiences, or discovering common interests, these insights can strengthen bonds and promote collaboration. Let us embark on this journey together, recognizing the beauty and significance of patterns in all their forms. As we uncover these connections, we can contribute to a future rich with understanding, innovation, and meaningful progress. As we embrace the patterns that shape our lives, let us remain open to exploration and discovery. The world is filled with patterns waiting to be recognized, and by connecting the dots, we can unlock new pathways for innovation, creativity, and progress. As we move forward, let us harness the power of patterns to enrich our lives, inspire change, and contribute to a brighter future for all